# Its' Time

Inner verses

Prashant Mehta

BookLeaf Publishing

India | USA | UK

Made with ❤ on the BookLeaf Publishing Platform
www.bookleafpub.in
www.bookleafpub.com

# Dedication

*To all the people and places that have shaped this journey, adding colors, lessons, and memories to the ever-evolving tapestry of life. Each experience—big or small—has been a brushstroke in this phenomenal menagerie, making it richer, deeper, and more meaningful. This book is a tribute to those moments, voices, and landscapes that have left an imprint on my soul.*

# Preface

*It's Time: Inner Verses* is a journey into the depths of thought, where the known and the unknown converge in poetic rhythm. Each poem in this collection emerges from the inner crevices of the mind—silent reflections, unspoken emotions, and fleeting moments that linger long after they pass. These verses are not just words; they are echoes of introspection, raw and unfiltered, capturing the essence of time, memory, and existence. This book is an invitation to pause, feel, and explore the emotions that often go unnoticed. May these poems resonate with the quiet corners of your soul.

# Acknowledgements

*This collection, It's Time: Inner Verses, would not have been possible without the love, support, and inspiration of those around me. I am deeply grateful to my **wife**, whose unwavering belief in me fuels my creativity, and to my **mother and daughter**, who bring beauty and meaning to my life. My **sisters**, with their warmth and laughter, add richness to this journey. A heartfelt thanks to all the people and places that have shaped my thoughts, leaving imprints that found their way into these verses. To my readers—thank you for embracing these words and making them your own.*

# 1. The Nature of Joy

When it comes to joy, I often ponder,
Is it fleeting, or does it wander?

Is it the glow when the sun peeps in,
Or the warmth from food where love has been?

Is it the thrill as I race downhill,
On a rickety bike with a reckless will?

Or the fear that gripped me tight,
When I dared a bull with all my might?

Whatever joy is, one truth remains,
It's both common and personal in different domains.

Personal, when it strikes me deep,
Common, when in shared laughter or weep.

Finding joy in a common space,
Is easier than in a lonely place.

But joy that's mine alone is strange,
For it often walks with pain in exchange.

Pain—when kept unshared,
Lingers like a wound impaired.

So what is joy—can we define?
Is it only ours, or something divine?

Or is it only real when it grows,
Passed from hand to hand, like a river that flows?

One thing is sure—it never stays,
It dances, spreads, in endless ways.

I've learned this in my years on earth,
That joy expands when given birth.

# 2. A Quest for Joy

But then I wondered, what if I'm alone?
Would joy still reach me on its own?
So I set sail, leaving land behind,
On a boat, to see what I'd find.
The ocean whispered, wild and free,
A restless tide calling to me.
Darkness fell, the waters churned,
My stomach fluttered, my courage burned.
Was this a dream? A fleeting trance?
Or the start of fate's new dance?
No, it was real—the salt, the spray,
The endless waves that dared me to stay.
The boat was small, the storm was vast,
I held the rudder, I gripped it fast.
Why had I left my home so bright,
For endless waters, void of light?
I thought of an island deep in the sea,
A place untouched, just for me.
I rowed, I steered, till the waves grew mild,
Till palms appeared, serene and wild.

An island! Alone at last, I beamed,
This was the joy I had once dreamed.
But then the rain poured, fierce and cold,
The soil was drenched, the night took hold.
No fire, no shelter, just me and the dark,
No comfort, no warmth, no friendly spark.
Was this the joy I longed to claim?
Or had my quest been lost in vain?
Joy, I thought, is not just a place,
Not just a moment, not just a chase.
It is shared, it is known, it is given away,
It is found in others, in night and in day.
And so I stood, soaked and wise,
With newfound truth beneath the skies.
Joy is not in solitude's embrace,
But in the love of a familiar face.

# 3. In Search of Recognition

I wandered far in search of name,
A flicker of light, a touch of fame.


Words poured forth, wild and free,
Yet none would listen, none would see.


Unpublished lines, raw yet true,
Drenched in ink, but lost from view.


My heart beat fast, both bright and heavy,
Torn between hope and nights unsteady.


Falling deep, yet rising tall,
Each verse a triumph, each a fall.


Still, my pen refused to rest,
Aching, yearning, giving its best.


Would my words find a place to stay?
Or fade like whispers swept away?

Pages aged, murky and musty,
Thoughts once bold, now torn and rusty.

Yet they lived, they gasped, they breathed,
Wove their pain, yet never seethed.

Mingling, drifting, lost yet found,
Echoing whispers without a sound.

They made me weak, they made me strong,
They chained me down, yet pulled me along.

Each syllable, each silent cry,
A piece of me that refused to die.

So I write—not for glory, not for gain,
Not for claps or fleeting fame.

But because the words, they call to me,
And in their whispers, I am free.

# 4. A Fault at Heart

I always thought, as I looked her way,
A fleeting glimpse, yet bound to stay.

Missed or noticed, lost or found,
Still, her shadow lingered around.

It felt so strange, yet stayed so true,
A silent ache that only grew.

Through shifting years, through nights untold,
Her scent, her flicker—warm yet cold.

It touched, it brushed, a ghostly trace,
Never fading, yet lost in space.

Not daunting, not ashamed,
Yet craving, longing, unrestrained.

From the crevices of my soul,
It surged, it slipped, it took control.

Died once, then lived again,
In ashes turned to fire's reign.

The blood, the pulse, the mind's embrace,
A love unseen, yet carved in place.

A whisper, a spark, a fleeting sign,
A moment lost yet still divine.

It faltered, wavered, yet remained,
Unspoken, raw, yet never feigned.

A glance from shadows, a look from skies,
Pain dissolves, yet never dies.

She is there—within, beyond,
In me, around—a tethered bond.

Here or nowhere, near or far,
A fault at heart, an unseen scar.

# 5. Invisible Him

He is unseen, yet I feel Him near,
A whisper, a shadow, a voice unclear.

They call Him God, yet when I see,
The face I find is only me.

Who else could He be, if not inside?
The stronger, the weaker, the fear, the pride.

The light that lifts, the dark that drowns,
The king with no throne, the beggar with crowns.

What happens when He looks at me?
A mirror reflects—am I what I see?

I groan, I glimmer, I rise, I fall,
A fleeting shade, yet part of it all.

Piercing through, it strips me bare,
A force unseen, yet always there.

Sadness peeks, then fades away,
Hope steps in, demanding to stay.

Something dims, something brightens,
A flickering ember that never frightens.

It fails, it falters, yet comes anew,
Like dawn's embrace in morning dew.

Like the hand of solace, steady and strong,
Like a father's pride, where I belong.

Not above, not beyond, but within my soul,
An unseen presence that makes me whole.

I search for Him, yet here I stand,
Not in temples, nor in sand.

Not in stars, nor skies above,
But in myself, in life, in love.

# 6. Blood, Blade, and Fate

Sitting at the table, lost in thought,
I pondered Salman, Rushdie's lot.

What did he feel when the blade tore through,
His neck, his eyes—did he ever knew?

A refugee, rich yet outcast still,
Lecherous? Ungodly? A fate to fulfill?

The same with Monica Seles, her silent scream,
A knife that shattered a champion's dream.

Violence speaks in tongues unknown,
A hand, a thought—it's never alone.

The blade that cleaves, the blood that flows,
Where does it end? Nobody knows.

Are they dead, or do they breathe?
In body slain, yet words still seethe.

Protected more from what they fear,
Yet haunted still by whispers near.

The knife, the push, the deed is done,
But does the war end with one?

Fresh bodies fall, more rise to stand,
The cycle turns, a shifting sand.

What pacifies—the death or life?
The silent grave or endless strife?

What remains when all is gone?
The stain of blood, the will to move on?

Does the knife truly end a tale?
Or does the pain forever prevail?

The living live, the dead stay dead,
Yet names remain where blood was shed.

The hand that struck, the mind that thought,
The endless battle—but what is sought?

It kills, it kills, and kills again,
But till when, till when, till when?

No one wins, no life is spared,
As death defies, yet none are prepared.

For life itself is just a chance,
A fleeting shadow—a dying dance.

# 7. The Chains of the Mind

He stood so tall, fierce and wide,
Yet shrank to nothing when sorrow cried.

But sorrow never touched his face,
So he loomed, a giant, in his place.

Like the moon, his size would shift,
Never still, a ceaseless drift.

I watched, I wondered, I felt so small,
Why did he matter to me at all?

A family man, just one of many,
Yet his presence felt too heavy.

Why did fear creep in his wake?
Why did I tremble, why did I break?

Why did I feel bound when he was near,
Yet weighed down more when he disappeared?

Was the weight in the chain, or in my mind?
Oh, **brother, tell me—what did I find?**

I forged my chains, link by link,
Bound by thoughts, afraid to think.

But why? For what? What sense was there,
When nothing is meant to be held in snare?

Who says man is born free, yet chained?
No, **no chains for me remain!**

I chain the sun, the stars, the sky,
Only in thought—so why should I cry?

The chains dissolve, the walls collapse,
The weight was never his to clasp.

He was not the cage, not the key,
For now I see—**he was me.**

And now I know, now I am free,
No chains remain—only **me.**

# 8. The Veins of Argument

Arguments are scary, fierce and loud,
Drenched in wisdom, wrapped in shroud.

Fake and real, yet never clear,
A battle of minds, a dance of fear.

They rise like storms, they twist, they turn,
Leaving hearts to ache and burn.

Some bring truth, some bring lies,
Yet all leave echoes in weary sighs.

They shake the soul, they clog the mind,
A bitter taste, a tie that binds.

Yet in their clash, what do we gain?
Logic may stand, but does it remain?

Does the victor truly win?
Or does the loss begin within?

I lost, yet joy was mine,
For in that fall, I saw the sign.

Losing made me softer, wise,
A pathfinder with clearer skies.

Yet I cried when I lost too,
For the wound was deep and fresh to view.

Is this all that life's about,
Where death is certain, life a doubt?

Do we fight just to be right,
Or do we wander, lost in spite?

What sense remains in walking tense,
Despising words with no defense?

For what is logic if hearts still bleed,
And doubts take root like tangled weeds?

It clears the thought, yet leaves a stain,
A cycle of loss, a loop of pain.

That's what arguments seem to be—
A vein of fire, wild yet free.

# 9. Whispers of the Silent Night: A Cry Unheard

When I cry in the depth of night,
Silent tears, yet strong in might.

It all flows out, yet in vain,
A hollow echo, no real gain.

I wonder why this pain must stay,
To suffer so much and not decay.

A battle lost before it's fought,
Yet I endured, yet I thought.

It seemed as if I ran away,
But I was trapped in sorrow's sway.

Crying for reasons lost in air,
Now dying seasons, none aware.

I once believed I was a spark,

Yet brilliance faded in the dark.

Why did fate play tricks so cruel,
Forcing hands, ignoring rule?

Was this the life we longed to find,
A fleeting breath, a restless mind?

It's not that I agreed or played,
It was never my choice—never my say.

Now the sun of time drips down,
Like fading echoes in a ghostly town.

It's dark, yet if you dare to see,
Perhaps you'll find what's meant to be.

For this is not just mine alone,
But every heart that weeps unknown.

The living, the lost, the ones who grieve,
The broken souls who still believe.

# 10. The Birds of My Childhood

I saw a morning bird one day,
Chirping softly in the sun's first ray.

By my window, perched so light,
Dusky feathers, a rickety sight.

Yet its song was pure and bright,
I listened, lost in golden light.

As my eyes began to drift,
Dreams and memories started to lift.

I wandered deep in slumber's haze,
To a time of reckless days.

There were more birds, singing loud,
Yet I stood there, young and proud.

I saw myself—a child so small,

Throwing stones to watch them fall.

Angry wings took to flight,
Chasing me with all their might.

I ran, but they were swift and free,
While little legs slowed down in plea.

I tripped and tumbled to the ground,
A ditch embraced, no help was found.

Above me, wings began to hover,
Mocking voices made me shudder.

*"Meet us when you're forty,"* they said,
Strange words whispered in my head.

Years passed, the garden's gone,
Walls surround where light once shone.

Yet outside, the birds still stay,
Silent watchers in their way.

Déjà vu—this scene, this tune,
Sunlight dull in my dim-lit room.

The same old birds, their piercing eyes,

A haunting song, no more disguise.

I long to play, to run once more,
To chase them like I did before.

I close my eyes, but time won't bend,
The birds are gone—so is my friend.

# 11. The Silent Guardians

When I see the trees—so vast, so free,
Swaying long in the windy spree.

They whisper stories, bold and deep,
Through skies where golden sunrays creep.

Green and grey, dark and dim,
Their mighty presence, firm and grim.

Standing tall, their roots embrace,
The earth's warm heart, a sacred space.

By day they toil, by night they rest,
Breathing life in nature's quest.

As the sun blazes, fierce and bright,
They cool the world in silent might.

Their shade holds tales of days gone by,
As souls depart into the sky.

The birds, the bees, the buzzing flies,
All dance beneath their leafy guise.

They guard my secrets, soft and true,
Listening as I cry anew.

Their breath—pure whispers in the air,
A touch of peace beyond compare.

I love the trees—not for their speech,
But for the lessons they quietly teach.

They never run, they never stray,
Yet stand beside me, come what may.

# 12. The Mountain That Once Was

I saw the mountains again today,
They stand still, yet not the same way.

Not like the ones of childhood past,
At Nani's home, where time held fast.

Back then, they loomed—so firm, so wide,
Where train tracks curved along their side.

Dull yet shining, sturdy and small,
A mountain dwarf, yet proud and tall.

Dynamites roared, the echoes spread,
Chipping away its rugged head.

Now it's gone—no roots, no crest,
Once alive, now laid to rest.

Forty years ago, it teemed with life,
Scorpions lurked, the dusk was rife.

Bushy trails and eerie calls,
Yet we were brave, we feared no falls.

Nani packed our secret share,
Food wrapped tight with quiet care.

We played till the sun had set,
Forgotten hours, no regrets.

As night grew cold, we turned around,
And scurried home without a sound.

Nani's warmth, her shield, her grace,
Kept mother's anger in its place.

The mountains stood, untouched, untamed,
A world beyond what hands had claimed.

But now, today, I found one near,
Familiar, yet it shook with fear.

No dynamite, no ruthless hand,
Yet sand slipped softly through my grasp.

Brittle, broken, barely there,
A fragile ghost in thinning air.

What have we made? What have we lost?
I stood in silence, counting the cost.

This was not my mountain bright,
The one that met my childhood sight.

# 13. The Paradox of Water...

The beauty of the ocean—vast, untold,
A whispering beast, fierce and bold.

Its gentle froth, a child at play,
Yet turns to wrath in a tidal sway.

I fear the ocean, deep and wild,
A restless force, untamed, beguiled.

Its surface shivers, dark and cold,
A trembling tale of powers old.

If what is written comes to be,
And waters rise to swallow me,

Will I drift or will I drown,
When all the world is waterbound?

*"Water, water everywhere, but not a drop to drink,"*
How true the words, how close the brink.


It bathes, it dirties, it purifies,
Yet in its depth, the lost soul lies.


Mix it, taint it, cleanse it whole,
It takes it all—it bears no toll.


And when the time is at its crest,
It swallows all—both cursed and blessed.


What makes us pure—just water's touch?
Or sacred streams we trust so much?


Ganges flowing, Zam Zam blessed,
Do they cleanse the soul at rest?


So scarce, so vast, so much to spare,
Yet wars are waged for drops laid bare.


I fear water—the sea untamed,
Salty, ruthless, never named.


And yet the sip within my glass,
Resting still, yet first and last.

I ask it soft, a quiet plea,
Forgive my sins, oh let me be.

For it gives life and death alike,
A fleeting drop, a drowning strike.

Do I drink it—or does it drink me?
The years will tell, the tides will see.

# 14. The Enigma of Earth...

What is Earth? I ask once more,
A drifting speck, a cosmic shore?

A world among the countless spread,
Or the place where fleeting lives are bred?

The soil, the trees, the beasts, the air,
A gift we take, yet leave threadbare.

Is Earth but life, both small and vast,
Or just a shadow, fading fast?

Perhaps a chimera, wild yet deep,
That makes my pain take root and creep.

It was there the day I came to be,
And will remain when I cease to see.

But till when? How long will it stay?
Are we alone, or led astray?

Does some great hand, unseen, unknown,
Guide our fate or leave us prone?

We search in books, in stars, in dust,
Yet mysteries twist and break our trust.

For every answer, countless rise,
Truth dissolves before our eyes.

But silence speaks, the soil stays,
The dust of time in golden rays.

The Earth, so soiled, so worn, so free,
Sold to us in bits—oh, irony.

From Earth to Mars, from then to now,
We chase the void, yet wonder how.

Shall we survive another fall,
While gods above watch over all?

Smiling, knowing, from afar,
We search for truths not where they are.

Not there, not here, not lost nor found,
But deep within—where I am bound.

# 15. The Fire Within

I spoke to my fire that once burned bright,
But found it cold—devoid of light.

I fanned, I begged, I called its name,
Yet it remained—a dying flame.

Dingy embers, smut-stained ash,
No flicker, no spark, no fiery clash.

I showed it flames that roared outside,
Still, it slumbered, dead inside.

Then anger surged, a tempest wild,
I asked my fire, fierce and riled—

*"If you stay cold, how shall I fight?*
*How shall I stand, bold in the night?"*

Fire stared with hollow eyes,
A void of silence, dark as skies.

I barked aloud, I dared, I swore,
*"Will you rise, or burn no more?"*


*"Fire without fire is no fire,"*
I taunted, urging its lost desire.


*"Why do you slumber, why so still?*
*Do you not long to burn with will?"*


It simmered low, it whispered death,
A soul at peace, untouched by breath.


*"I seek no rage, no mindless spree,*
*My depth is where I'm meant to be."*


I pleaded, I crumbled, I fought in vain,
As silence met me once again.


*"If you are my fire, yet burn no more,*
*What will become of my soul's core?"*


And then it asked, quiet but strong,
*"Why do you need fire at all?"*


Without its heat, how could I strive?
Without its spark, how would I thrive?

I would not just survive, not yet, not now,
I must rise, I must know how.

And so I swore, through dimming light,
*"One more try—I will ignite."*

# 16. The Ice That Burned

The ice I held within my hand,
Did not numb—it took a stand.

It burned a hole, so vast, so wide,
A silent wound I could not hide.

I crushed it tight, yet burned it more,
A searing chill down to my core.

This was not my fire's embrace,
But icy cold—a frozen place.

Was this the will I longed to own?
To beg, to borrow, make it known?

To burn, yet freeze—both fire and frost,
A paradox, a will near lost.

A cold heat simmered deep inside,
Yet ice refused to slip or slide.

No sun could melt, no warmth could break,
It stood like steel—no give, no quake.

*"Why?"* I asked, *"What holds you still?*
*Why do you defy the nature's will?"*

It met my gaze with frozen breath,
And whispered low, *"You walk with death."*

*"Your fire's gone, your warmth is dead,*
*And so with you, I freeze instead."*

# 17. The Whisper of Air...

Air that breathes me, and I breathe too,
Silent, unseen, yet ever true.

Calm it seems, a fleeting guest,
Yet I stood before its force—oppressed.

A jet of air, so fierce, so wide,
Left me breathless, lost inside.

Did it steal the life from me,
Or give it back, wild and free?

I wondered then, what if none came?
No whisper soft, no wisp, no name.

I saw the breathless grasp and fade,
As panic wove its silent blade.

Yet in the air, a secret lies,
A hope that soars, a fear that sighs.

It lingers there, so light, so thin,
A touch unseen, yet deep within.

They say it holds both love and fear,
A force so vast, yet ever near.

It beckons me, yet stays apart,
A ghostly hand upon my heart.

And still, I shun what gives me life,
For never seen, yet ever rife.

But what is rare is ever dear,
And air is all—so close, so clear.

# 18. The Jungle Within...

The eyes of darkness peered through the deep,
A jungle thick, where secrets sleep.

Off the road, beyond the vale,
A place where whispers tell their tale.

I stepped inside, alone, untamed,
With thoughts that flickered, wild, unnamed.

Old trees loomed, they watched me pass,
Like ancient monks of stone and grass.

A hermit's walk, a seeker's dream,
Was I to find some truth unseen?

Like Buddha once, who walked this path,
Seeking light in shadows vast.

*"Buddha?"*—I stopped, I felt the shame,
To utter lightly such a name.

But then a voice within me said,
*"You are Brahman, pure, unshed."*

Not of caste, nor bound by creed,
But a spark of God, a soul set free.

Then came a bee, like molten gold,
Racing fast, so swift, so bold.

I ducked, I tripped, I fell to dust,
The jungle breathed—its breath robust.

I searched behind, but none was there,
Yet fear had stirred the silent air.

*"Why am I here?"*—the thought returned,
Was this a place for truth to burn?

The jungle, old, knew me so young,
Yet to its time, I was still undone.

Why did Buddha seek the trees?
Why does the seeker chase the breeze?

I thought again, and I was freed—
I am Brahman, no lesser seed.

But do I wish to be the one,
Who sits beneath a setting sun?

A Bodhisattva in the leaves,
Or one whom restless time deceives?

Where is my tree?—I do not know,
For trees have ants, and bites, and woe.

*"You think too much of flesh and bone,"*
My mind had whispered, cold as stone.

*"Perhaps another life,"* it said,
*"But why are you here instead?"*

A fad, a folly, a fleeting flight,
A jungle walk, an endless night.

It darkened fast, the noises grew,
Cold leaves clung, the branches blew.

The jungle knew, it always did,
And in its eyes, I was still a kid.

Escape, escape—but from what, from whom?
A question circled in the gloom.

I climbed the tree, to bide the night,
Perhaps tomorrow would bring me light.

# 19. The Lake and the Narcissus Farewell...

I gazed upon the still lake's face,
Like Narcissus, lost in its embrace.

But stillness fled as ripples spread,
Some unseen hand, some pebble sped.

I turned to see—yet none was there,
Save for a tree with watchful stare.

Its branches swayed, its pollen fell,
Disturbing waters, breaking the spell.

I let it pass—I held no might,
To tame the wind, to halt its flight.

Yet in the ripples, in the dance,
My face was split in liquid trance.

A bird nearby began to sing,

A melody of fleeting wings.

Yet I remained, my eyes confined,
To waves that fractured all I'd divined.

Then darkness loomed, a shadow spread,
A cloud above—so vast, so dread.

The lake grew restless, pollen thick,
The golden light was gone so quick.

The wind had roared, the bird had fled,
And fear replaced what peace had bred.

Yet in the storm, in wrath so wide,
I saw a beauty, fierce with pride.

A force divine, a fleeting flame,
Was it God, or just a name?

The cloud, enraged, with thunder spoke,
And spat its fire—but silence broke.

I leapt beneath a clustered tree,
Anticipating destiny.

But fate was fickle, swift, unkind—

The storm had passed, left naught behind.

Back to the lake, where waters dim,
Reflected not, but only grim.

The tree once proud, now torn in two,
A broken raft in murky blue.

The bird stayed gone, the wind grew thin,
And something stilled my heart within.

I left the lake, the sky turned wide,
And bid farewell to Narcissus' pride.

# 20. The Silent Shame!

I remember well, that fleeting day,
Pedaling fast on a sunlit way.

The cycle's chain had slipped aside,
Grease-stained hands, nowhere to hide.

No cloth, no water, nothing near,
Just open lands, both bright and clear.

Then there it stood—a plant so fine,
Velvety leaves in silent shine.

Without a thought, without a care,
I wiped my hands—my burden shared.

The grease had gone, but at a cost,
Something pure had now been lost.

And as I rode, a sudden sting,
A weight of guilt came lingering.

I turned to look—those petals bright,
Now smeared in black, yet held no fight.

No cry, no scorn, no anger cast,
Yet shame within me held steadfast.

It felt as if, with careless hands,
I'd wronged a child who never demands.

Forty years have passed since then,
Yet still it glows in memory's den.

A moment small, a lesson vast,
That silent voices speak the past.

And in my mind, I see them yet,
Those angry petals, stained and set.

Saying nothing, bearing all,
Yet echoing still—my silent fall.

# 21. The End That Never Ends

The end is inevitable, that we know,
But how it comes, when it will show—

Will it be like the reckless wasp,
Drawn to fire in one last gasp?

Or like the crow, in careless flight,
That meets its fate in tangled light?

Or the lion, once bold and grand,
Who falls when strength slips from its hand?

Or is it like the sun at dusk,
Fading slow, yet built on trust?

To set, to rise, to start once more,
A cycle spinning evermore.

Certainty—we chase, we crave,

Mapping the stars, escaping the grave.

We mark the moon, we chart the Mars,
Yet still we're trapped among the stars.

Does it end? Or does it pass—
A flickered torch, a fleeting glass?

Each death a spark, a fire anew,
A whispered breath that life pursues.

The wasp returns, the light still glows,
Through endless dark, the ember flows.

Again, again—it fights, it flies,
Till death is false and time belies.

For what we call the final breath,
Is but a pause, not bound to death.

And what appears to break, descend—
May just begin where others end.